Daily English Expressions (2)

(Speak English Lika a Native)

Forward

The English Language is like any other language full of expressions and idiomatic vocabulary that need to be addressed adequately and correctly to gain mastery of this language. Besides, it is a matter of both locating and pinpointing the right material as well as the right style that are likely to fit in with our learning style which eventually enables us to make progress in the learning process.

Daily English Expressions is a carefully selected sets of common vocabulary, phrases, idioms and phrasal verbs that are sure to make a real difference in your ability to communicate in English. These expressions are presented through interactive English contexts with examples extracted directly from daily life situations.

If your target is to speak fluently and gain confidence in English, go ahead and take a crack at this book - success is guaranteed.

Table of Contents

Chapter (1) 4
Expressions (1 – 10)

Chapter (2) 11
Expressions (11 – 20)

Chapter (3) 18
Expressions (21 – 30)

Chapter (4) 25
Expressions (31 – 40)

Chapter (5) 32
Expressions (41 – 50)

Chapter (6) 39
Expressions (51 – 60)

Chapter (7) 46
Expressions (61 – 70)

Chapter (8) 53
Expressions (71 – 80)

Chapter (9) 60
Expressions (81 – 90)

Chapter (10) 67
Expressions (91 – 100)

List of Expressions 74

Chapter 1

Expressions (1 – 10)

1. appalling

Situation 1:

A: *I can't get over the way Jack behaved at your party - it was **appalling**!*
B: *I agree. His lack of manners is quite **appalling**.*

Situation 2:

A: *You don't seem to have had a good time at the new restaurant.*
B: *Yep. The meal was a rip-off and the service was **appalling**.*

Definition: (adjective) awful or horrible, causing dismay or disgust.

2. appealing

Situation 1:

A: *Wow! Sounds like you're excited about the new job.*
B: *The idea of not having to get up early every morning is rather **appealing** (to me).*

Situation 2:

A: *Who do you suggest we can assign to give the talk on behalf of the board?*
B: *I think Pete is cut out for this task. He has a nice smile and an **appealing** personality.*

Definition: (adjective) pleasing and attractive.

3. serve a purpose

Situation 1:

A: *So, how are we going to remove the weeds form the garden?*
B: *Unfortunately, we don't have a spading fork but this shovel should* **serve the purpose**!

Situation 2:

A: *Why don't you throw out these old tyres?*
B: *Well, I keep them because they* **serve a purpose**. *I use them as a fence to prevent the stray animals from destroying my garden.*

Definition: to be useful for or fit to achieve some aim, goal, or purpose.

4. up-and-coming

Situation 1:

A: *Is it a wise decision to buy a property in a remote place like this?*
B: *This is an* **up-and-coming** *area. Hundreds of businesses are investing in here.*

Situation 2:

A: *Isn't Tyson too young to lead the committee?*
B: *Not at all. He's an* **up-and-coming** *executive with a bright future.*

Definition: (adjective) likely to achieve success in the near future.

5. down-to-earth

Situation 1:

A: *Do you get along with your new manager?*
B: *Absolutely. She's a **down-to-earth** sort of woman with no pretensions.*

Situation 2:

A: *This arrogant approach is alienating your employees. You need to win them if you want them to be more productive.*
B: *Maybe you're right. I should try to be more **down-to-earth**.*

Definition: (adjective) practical and direct in dealing with people.

6. edgy

Situation 1:

A: *Come on, Pete. It's not very nice of you to leave our guest on her own!*
B: *She is talking too much. I am getting so **edgy** I might scream at her.*

Situation 2:

A: *I'm feeling a bit **edgy** about the exam tomorrow.*
B: *Relax. You've revised well for it, there's nothing to worry about.*

Definition: (adjective) tense, nervous, or irritable.

7. single out

Situation 1:

A: *I never learned why the principals **singled me out** to receive this gift.*
B: *You deserved it. That's all.*

Situation 2:

A: *I still don't understand why the bullies **singled** Michael **out** from all other boys!*
B: *Typically, bullies **single out** the smallest or the quietest.*

Definition: to choose and focus on a single person or thing out of a group of others.

8. stock up on (something)

Situation 1:

A: *Why are you **stocking up on** all these canned foods?*
B: *I don't like to cook.*

Situation 2:

A: *You buy good quality products with reasonable prices. What's your secret?*
B: *I compare everyday prices and plan my shopping accordingly to **stock up on** the best priced products.*

Definition: to buy a large amount of something so that you will have enough for the future.

9. behave oneself

Situation 1:

A: *What do I have to do to let me in?*
B: ***Behave yourself*** *and keep quiet.*

Situation 2:

A: *I won't help you organize the party unless you get me a red scarf.*
B: *Talk sense and **behave yourself**. You are not a kid anymore.*

Definition: to act in a polite or proper way.

10. hard up

Situation 1:

A: *We're a bit **hard-up** at the moment so we're not thinking about vacations.*
B: *Good thinking.*

Situation 2:

A: *My salary isn't sufficient and I'm always short of money.*
B: *Don't complain of being **hard up** before me!*

Definition: (adjective) not to have enough money; short of money.

Measure your progress

<u>Fill in the gaps with the missing words;</u>

1. Many up-and-……….. young players have trials for the national football team.

2. For some reason, the bullies keep singling me ……….. to pick on each day.

3. Your suggestion is ……….. in theory, but it lacks practicality.

4. Don't worry, I've been ……….. up on fuel for the past three years for just such an occasion.

5. He needs to marry a ………..-to-earth person who will organize his life for him.

6. She is always ……… up because she doesn't lay out her money wisely.

7. Nothing will change as long as the workers continue to accept these ……….. conditions.

8. The boys were grounded because they failed to ……….. themselves.

9. Sarah will get ……….. and defensive when someone mentions her family.

10. The player's versatility means that he can serve a ……….. in many positions on the pitch.

Answers;

1. coming   2. out   3. appealing   4. stocking   5. down
6. hard   7. appalling   8. behave   9. edgy   10. purpose

Chapter 2

Expressions (11 – 20)

11. grounded

Situation 1:

A: *That's not fair, mom. Why do you single me out for doing the cleaning?*
B: *You will be **grounded** for a week if you don't keep quiet. Understood?*

Situation 2:

A: *Where's Mike, the captain of the team?*
B: *Mike isn't playing today. My father said he's **grounded**.*

Definition: a child or young person who is grounded is not allowed to go out as a punishment.

12. good thinking

Situation 1:

A: *Why wait until they call? Let's take them by surprise and give them a ring.*
B: *Yes, we'll phone them instead – **good thinking**.*

Situation 2:

A: *It was **good thinking** to quit smoking before it ruins your health.*
B: *Honestly, health has little to do with this decision. I'm just hard up these days.*

Definition: that's a good idea or decision.

13. Call someone names

Situation 1:

A: *My son doesn't want to go to school because the kids are **calling him names.***
B: *You should go and see their principal to put a stop to it.*

Situation 2:

A: *Alice slapped Bernard and **called him names**, but he didn't react.*
B: *He can't because he's the guilty one.*

Definition: to insult somebody with rude or unpleasant names.

14. pick on someone

Situation 1:

A: *Hey, Sam. How long were you grounded last night?*
B: *Get out of here. Why don't you **pick on** someone your own size?*

Situation 2:

A: *Do you know why Sally decided to leave our school?*
B: *She was **picked on** by the other girls because of her size.*

Definition: to harass or bother someone or something, usually unfairly.

15. alienate

<u>**Situation 1**</u>:

A: *I'll invite all the department to a dinner party. What do you say?*
B: *Good thinking. We'd better not **alienate** ourselves from our colleagues.*

<u>**Situation 2**</u>:

A: *Watch out. Asking your customers to pay for delivery services will **alienate** most of them.*
B: *This is a makeshift plan. I'll replace it if it doesn't work.*

<u>**Definition**</u>: to cause (someone) to stop being friendly, helpful, etc., towards you.

16. cut out for (something)

<u>**Situation 1**</u>:

A: *I left medicine anyway. I wasn't really **cut out for** it.*
B: *That's what happens when people don't follow their passions. You're **cut out for** football – everybody knows that!*

<u>**Situation 2**</u>:

A: *Everybody voted for Mike as the representative of the class.*
B: *Mike's assertive personality qualifies him for this task. He's **cut out for** it.*

<u>**Definition**</u>: (adjective) to be suited for or capable of some activity or position.

17. designate as

Situation 1:

A: *There's a room left. Can we **designate** it **as** an office?*
B: *If you think it's appropriate, go ahead!*

Situation 2:

A: *We need to **designate** someone **as** the leader of the team.*
B: *Don't look at me! I'm not cut out for this job.*

Definition: to choose someone or something for a special job or purpose

18. lay the blame on

Situation 1:

A: *I feel bad because our colleagues got fired. Sarah convinced me to report what happened to the boss.*
B: *Don't **lay the blame on** anyone. You have to take responsibility for your mistakes.*

Situation 2:

A: *David **laid the blame** for the accident **on** the car. He said it was broken.*
B: *That's what everyone says when they don't find someone else to blame.*

Definition: to say or think that someone did something wrong.

19. hamper

Situation 1:

A: *I heard Mary was mugged last night.*
B: *Yeah, she tried to run when the mugger stopped her, but was **hampered** by her heavy suitcase.*

Situation 2:

A: *The hens are not laying enough eggs!*
B: *Freezing weather in spring **hampers** the hens' ability to lay eggs.*

Definition: to make it difficult for someone to do something.

20. bounce back

Situation 1:

A: *I'm starting to worry about Tom's condition after he lost the competition.*
B: *Don't worry. He is young enough to **bounce back** from this disappointment.*

Situation 2:

A: *Is Mary's injury completely healed?*
B: *Not yet; but the doctors expect her to **bounce back** and make a full recovery.*

Definition: to return quickly to a normal condition after a difficult situation or event.

Measure your progress

<u>**Fill in the gaps with the missing words;**</u>

1. It was no good .... to let Sarah go home alone at this late time.

2. I stayed out till 1 am last night and now I'm .... for a week.

3. Bill's tendency to make silly remarks .... his roommates.

4. Sam is still a life guard - he's just not .... out for a nine-to-five job.

5. They laid the .... on the waiter for the spilled soup.

6. The officer .... some customers as watchmen during the investigation.

7. After beating him three times in a row, David was so angry that he began calling them ....

8. Liverpool's footballers hope to .... back after their defeat in Europe last week.

9. The search was .... by appalling weather conditions.

10. The kids at school pick .... him for wearing glasses.

Answers;

1. thinking   2. grounded   3. alienated   4. cut   5. blame
6. designated   7. names   8. bounce   9. hampered   10. on

Chapter 3

Expressions (21 – 30)

21. makeshift

Situation 1:

A: *How did you manage to survive the snowstorm?*
B: *We built a **makeshift** shelter under the trees.*

Situation 2:

A: *So, you stayed in your office for two months straight when you started the business. How did you sleep?*
B: *Actually, I set up a **makeshift** bed and slept behind my desk.*

Definition: (adjective) temporary and of low quality, but used because of a sudden need.

22. (not) lift a finger

Situation 1:

A: *Why did you break up with your roommate?*
B: *He just watches TV and never **lifts a finger** to help with the chores.*

Situation 2:

A: *Did you carry all these boxes on your own?*
B: *Yeah. Joe **didn't lift a finger** to help with the move.*

Definition: make the slightest effort to do something, especially to help someone.

23. go for (something or someone) – 1 -

<u>**Situation 1**</u>:

A: *Daniel; I'm stopping by the supermarket. What kind of ice cream do you want?*
B: *Well, I'll **go for** the vanilla ice cream.*

<u>**Situation 2**</u>:

A: *Did you get that fancy phone we saw in the shop last week?*
B: *No. I spent half of my money on the roof repairs, so I just **went for** a basic phone in the end.*

<u>**Definition**</u>: to choose something or someone.

24. go for (something or someone) – 2 -

<u>**Situation 1**</u>:

A: *What sort of movies do you **go for**?*
B: *I'm a big fan of action movies.*

<u>**Situation 2**</u>:

A: *Mike is so handsome. Why didn't you like him?*
B: *He's not really my type – I don't usually **go for** arrogant guys.*

<u>**Definition**</u>: to find someone or something interesting or desirable.

25. (get) mad at someone

<u>**Situation 1**</u>:

A: *Did you tell Dad that I scratched up his car?*
B: *Of course not. He'll **get mad at** both of us.*

<u>**Situation 2**</u>:

A: *Are you still **mad at** me?*
B: *Yes, I am. I won't talk to you unless you fix what you've spoiled.*

<u>**Definition**</u>: to be angry at or with someone.

26. lost in thought

<u>**Situation 1**</u>:

A: *So, what do you think of this plan – shall I go for it?*
B: *Sorry; I didn't hear a word you said, I was **lost in thought**.*

<u>**Situation 2**</u>:

A: *Do you find your math classes engaging?*
B: *I don't know – I'm **lost in thought** most of the time during class.*

<u>**Definition**</u>: giving all your attention to what you are thinking about and not noticing what is going on around you.

27. no thanks to

<u>**Situation 1**</u>:

A: *I'm sorry; Jane. I wasn't able to lend you the money. I had to close an important deal.*
B: *It's OK. I managed to solve my problem,* **no thanks to you**.

<u>**Situation 2**</u>:

A: *I passed the exam,* **no thanks to** *my math teacher.*
B: *Come on, Dave. Don't be so ungrateful. The man did his best in class.*

<u>**Definition**</u>: without any help from someone or something.

28. set off

<u>**Situation 1**</u>:

A: *We've been riding for three hours straight. Are you hungry, guys?*
B: *Not yet. We ate a hearty breakfast before we* **set off**.

<u>**Situation 2**</u>:

A: *What time will you* **set off** *for school tomorrow?*
B: *At seven sharp.*

<u>**Definition**</u>: to start a journey, or to start going in a particular direction.

29. back off

<u>**Situation 1**</u>:

A: *I'm here to say that I'll stand by you in this crisis.*
B: *Just **back off** and let us do this on our own, will you?*

<u>**Situation 2**</u>:

A: *Nobody is willing to listen to me at home. They're just fighting each other all the time.*
B: *I think you should **back off** for a while.*

<u>Definition</u>: to stop being involved in a situation, usually in order to allow other people to deal with it themselves.

30. written all over someone's face

<u>**Situation 1**</u>:

A: *How did you know that Steven had stolen the purse?*
B: *It was **written all over his face.***

<u>**Situation 2**</u>:

A: *I can tell you've got great news. It's **written all over your face.** Tell me what it is!*
B: *I've finally got my driving license.*

<u>Definition</u>: someone's face is showing their true feelings or thoughts.

Measure your progress

<u>**Fill in the gaps with the missing words;**</u>

1. The children never lift a ………….. to help around the house.

2. Offered the choice between a higher salary and more vacation time, I know which one I'd …….. for.

3. We get ……….. at each other sometimes, like any family.

4. I don't really go ……….. modern art. It's confusing and full of nonsense.

5. I got home by taxi, no ……….. to my old car.

6. They equipped themselves with a pair of sharp axes and set ……….. for the forest.

7. She started to criticize me, then she suddenly ……….. off.

8. He's got evil ………….. all over his face, and his eyes are bursting with pure demon.

9. We turned the box upside down and used it as a ……….. table.

10. He didn't respond for a few moments, his gaze on the wall behind me, as if ……….. in thought.

Answers;

1. finger   2. go   3. mad   4. for   5. thanks
6. off   7. backed   8. written   9. makeshift   10. lost

Chapter 4

Expressions (31 – 40)

31. engaging

<u>**Situation 1**</u>:

A: *James seems to be pleased with his new school.*
B: *Right. His **engaging** personality made him popular with his peers.*

<u>**Situation 2**</u>:

A: *The **engaging** videos of our channel are obviously resonating with the viewers.*
B: *Absolutely. But you have to remember that creating this type of unique and **engaging** content is difficult and expensive.*

<u>Definition</u>: (adjective) tending to draw favorable attention or interest; attractive.

32. at all costs

<u>**Situation 1**</u>:

A: *I'll take a legal action against Anna if she refuses to return the jewelry.*
B: *Try not take it any further. Getting involved in a court case is something to be avoided **at all costs.***

<u>**Situation 2**</u>:

A: *The boss wants everyone to stay until seven.*
B: *I say "NO" **at all costs**.*

<u>Definition</u>: regardless of the difficulty or cost; no matter what.

33. touching

Situation 1:

A: *I couldn't watch the movie last night. Did I miss on much?*
B: *I frankly became rather absorbed in the story, which I found very* ***touching***.

Situation 2:

A: *You've been looking at this photo for a while. What do like about it?*
B: *The **touching** innocence of our daughter's eyes.*

Definition: (adjective) having a strong emotional effect; causing feelings of sadness or sympathy.

34. set up

Situation 1:

A: *I bought a new bike, but I'm not sure how to **set it up**.*
B: *Don't worry. I can give you hand.*

Situation 2:

A: *We need to **set up** a good schedule for taking the kids to school.*
B: *You take them early in the morning and I pick them up in the afternoon. I won't get up early at all costs.*

Definition: to assemble, organize, erect, or make ready for use.

35. rest assured

<u>**Situation 1**</u>:

A: *Did you make the necessary arrangement for our stay?*
B: *You can **rest assured** that all our needs will be taken care of at the hotel.*

<u>**Situation 2**</u>:

A: *Can I **rest assured** that I did not influence your decision with regard to this deal?*
B: *Of course, not. I'm totally convinced that I made the right decision.*

<u>**Definition**</u>: to be certain that something will happen.

36. wear something out

<u>**Situation 1**</u>:

A: *Not changing your engine oil regularly can **wear it out**.*
B: *Who cares? It's an old car, anyway!*

<u>**Situation 2**</u>:

A: *Don't rub your feet on the ground like that. No wonder you **wear out** your shoes in no time!*
B: *These aren't my shoes. They are Sam's!*

<u>**Definition**</u>: to cause to become damaged or eroded, as from frequent or rough use.

37. wear someone out

Situation 1:

A: *Correcting and sorting all these papers is **wearing you out**. I'll get you something to drink.*
B: *Thanks dear. You're the best.*

Situation 2:

A: *Standing all day has **worn me out**. My feet are sore and my back is stiff.*
B: *Well, go home and get some rest.*

Definition: to exhaust someone; to make someone tired.

38. worn-out

Situation 1:

A: *When I visited Samantha in hospital, she looked faded and **worn-out**.*
B: *Poor she. She lost half of hair family in a year.*

Situation 2:

A: *The sight of these **worn-out** socks is gross. Throw them out for heaven's sake.*
B: *I won't. They can still serve a purpose. I will use them to wipe the floor.*

Definition: extremely tired (someone) - too old or damaged to use (something).

39. give in (to something or someone)

<u>**Situation 1**</u>:

A: *Mary doesn't want to tell me who hides the files.*
B: *Keep asking and eventually she'll **give in**.*

<u>**Situation 2**</u>:

A: *Once you **give in** to temptation and eat fat, your program is going to be terminated.*
B: *Well, I don't mind strict rules as long as they are in my favor.*

<u>**Definition**</u>: cease fighting or arguing; admit defeat; to finally agree to what someone wants.

40. see eye to eye (on something)

<u>**Situation 1**</u>:

A: *What causes most of your arguments with your wife at home.*
B: *We simply don't **see eye to eye on** many issues, but usually I am the one who gives in.*

<u>**Situation 2**</u>:

A: *You'd be a fool to waste your time in doing what you hate when you have all the world before you.*
B: *I don't usually **see eye to eye** with you, but I'll do this.*

<u>**Definition**</u>: to share someone's position or opinion on some topic or issue.

Measure your progress

<u>**Fill in the gaps with the missing words;**</u>

1. You can rest ………… that we will do everything we can to get your money back.

2. Many teachers are dynamic, instructive, entertaining and skilled at presenting ……….. lectures.

3. He ………….. me out with his constant complaining.

4. You wheels will wear ………….. in no time if you keep overusing the brakes.

5. Derek nagged me so much for a new bike that eventually I ………….. in.

6. We must at all …………. prevent them from finding out about the plan.

7. My partner and I don't usually ………….. eye-to-eye but we manage to coexist.

8. The way she took care of her little sister was really ……….

9. A committee has been set ………….. to organize social events in the college.

10. You look …………..-out after your long journey.

Answers;

1. assured   2. engaging   3. wears   4. out   5. gave
6. costs   7. see   8. touching   9. up   10. worn

Chapter 5

Expressions (41 – 50)

41. nag (someone)

Situation 1:

A: *My mum's always **nagging** me to get my hair cut.*
B: *She's right. Those who want to have long hair need to take care of it, don't they?*

Situation 2:

A: *Oh, God. Everything is so calm in here away from home.*
B: *Yeah. The kids are no longer **nagging** you day and night.*

Definition: to keep asking or telling someone to do something.

42. not buy (something)

Situation 1:

A: *I know the boss is mad at me for not answering his calls, but I will tell him that I forgot the phone in the car.*
B: *I **don't** think he'll **buy your story**.*

Situation 2:

A: *The mechanic said that using new spare parts can wear out the other older parts in the car.*
B: *I don't think this is true. **I don't buy it.***

Definition: to not accept or believe something as the truth.

43. in good hands

Situation 1:

A: *The fees of this school are definitely beyond our means.*
B: *Probably, but at least we can be sure our children are **in good hands**.*

Situation 2:

A: *Where do you recommend I should do the repairs?*
B: *Go to the main garage and rest assured that your car will be **in good hands**.*

Definition: being well taken care of or managed very carefully.

44. resonate with

Situation 1:

A: *Wearing worn-looking clothing seems to **resonate with** young people.*
B: *This is a crazy passing fad. In fact, the idea of looking shabby never appealed to me.*

Situation 2:

A: *Did you tell Mark that we're selling the branch?*
B: *No, I didn't. But I did tell him that the work he proposed did not **resonate with me**.*

Definition: to relate harmoniously; to appeal to someone or cause someone to relate to it.

45. couch potato

Situation 1:

A: *Although Sam and Alfred are playing video games all the time, they have the skills we need to run a website.*
B: *Do you want me to work with those **couch potatoes**. I'd rather close the website than allow them to run it.*

Situation 2:

A: *What are you up to these days, Sam?*
B: *Actually, I'm becoming **couch potato** during football season.*

Definition: a person who takes little or no exercise and watches a lot of television.

46. sparingly

Situation 1:

A: *Go easy on the lotion, will you? The instructions say it should be applied **sparingly** to the skin.*
B: *Oops! Sorry, I didn't read them.*

Situation 2:

A: *Did you run out of water during the expedition?*
B: *No, we had plenty of it thanks to the guide who told us to use it **sparingly**.*

Definition: in a restricted or infrequent manner; in small quantities.

47. in the first place (1)

<u>**Situation 1**</u>:

A: *Why are you looking at me like that? Did I make any mistake?*
B: ***In the first place*** *it's not your house, and in the second nobody told you to do the dishes. Is that clear?*

<u>**Situation 2**</u>:

A: *Why do you think Suzan refused to go out on a date with me?*
B: ***In the first place*** *you are not old and in the second place you are a very attractive man.*

<u>**Definition**</u>: initially; to begin with. (used at the beginning of a sentence to introduce the different points you are making in an argument).

48. in the first place (2)

<u>**Situation 1**</u>:

A: *It was because of Derek that we winded up in the police station.*
B: *Why did you agree to meet him **in the first place**?*

<u>**Situation 2**</u>:

A: *Dave finally sold the house after he had failed to fund the necessary renovations.*
B: *He should have bought a new one **in the first place**.*

<u>**Definition:**</u> from the beginning. (used at the end of a sentence to talk about why something was done or whether it should have been done or not)

49. try one's hand (at something)

Situation 1:

A: *Pete, you're a famous painter. How did it all start?*
B: *I **tried my hand at** painting during my leisure and I eventually winded up a professional painter.*

Situation 2:

A: *You're taking an IT course, aren't you?*
B: *Yep. I'd like to **try my hand** at computing.*

Definition: to attempt to do something new; to try something for the first time.

50. cross (one's) path

Situation 1:

A: *Is it really bad luck if a black cat **crosses your path**?*
B: *Well, it depends on you. If you believe in this superstition, the answer is "yes".*

Situation 2:

A: *What if Dan and I hadn't **crossed paths** that particular evening, at that particular hour?*
B: *Thankfully, it happened. You two are a perfect match.*

Definition: to come into contact with someone or something, often surprisingly or unexpectedly.

Measure your progress

<u>Fill in the gaps with the missing words;</u>

1. We need to hire a competent lawyer to make sure that our company is in ………. hands.

2. Kathy's bossed and ……… me ever since we got married. Our life is a real hell.

3. The elder son is a bookworm while the younger one is a ……… potato.

4. I still don't understand why you chose that hilarious name in the ……… place.

5. Simon said he didn't see any of the reviews on the website but I don't ………. it.

6. In the first ……….., I'm too busy, and in the second I don't really want to go.

7. More than once, more than a dozen times I have been tempted to try my ………. at another profession.

8. Sally means nothing to me now. I hope I never cross her ……… again.

9. Dieticians recommend eating red meat ………. .

10. I am happy that I have found thousands of people who ………. with me, whose love, whose trust, is unconditionally with me.

Answers;

1. good   2. nagged   3. couch   4. first   5. buy
6. place   7. hand   8. path   9. sparingly   10. resonate

Chapter 6

Expressions (51 – 60)

51. whatsoever

<u>Situation 1</u>:

A: *Poor Albert. He lost half of his assets in a single deal!*
B: *He's had no luck **whatsoever**.*

<u>Situation 2</u>:

A: *Tom - what's the secret behind your agility?*
B: *I get enough sleep, I work out regularly, besides, I don't take any drugs **whatsoever**, except aspirin for colds.*

<u>Definition</u>: at all. (used after a negative phrase to add emphasis to the idea that is being expressed)

52. twice as much, many, etc.

<u>Situation 1</u>:

A: *That's all for today. You guys have to pick up your baskets and head home.*
B: *But the first basket has **twice as many fruits as** the second basket. That's not fair!*

<u>Situation 2</u>:

A: *Considering the quantity of ink we are producing now, we'll never make profits.*
B: *Once your computers start operating, we'll be able to produce **twice as much** at the same time.*

<u>Definition</u>: the quantity or the number of something is two times larger than another.

53. take something to the bank

<u>**Situation 1**</u>:

A: *I heard from a very reliable source that a wave of layoffs is looming —* ***you can take it to the bank.***
B: *Never mind. I have my back-up plans for such times.*

<u>**Situation 2**</u>:

A: *What's the point in studying if you don't make money whatsoever? I'll drop out of school.*
B: *Dear, son. You're not going to school to gain money, but to learn how to live adequately when you make money.* ***You can take that to the bank.***

<u>**Definition**</u>: that's definitely true.

54. compelling

<u>**Situation 1**</u>:

A: *Lucy had no **compelling** reason for not contacting us for three months.*
B: *I think she has. She has been in hospital since we met her last time.*

<u>**Situation 2**</u>:

A: *Do you think Mike is going to be released?*
B: *Certainly! The lawyer came across very compelling evidence, and he'll present it to the court tomorrow.*

<u>**Definition**</u>: convincing: very exciting and interesting and making you want to watch or listen.

55. all of a sudden

<u>**Situation 1**</u>:

A: *What's the matter? Why did you stop?*
B: *I felt a sharp pain in my side **all of a sudden.***

<u>**Situation 2**</u>:

A: *Greg is being very nice **all of a sudden**. What's his game?*
B: *He's destitute these days. You know, maybe he wants you to lend him some cash.*

<u>**Definition**</u>: unexpectedly and abruptly; suddenly.

56. more often than not

<u>**Situation 1**</u>:

A: *Rob was making enough money to get by, don't you think?*
B: *I don't think so. **More often than not** he came back to his apartment empty-handed.*

<u>**Situation 2**</u>:

A: *So, you claim you're an experienced chess player!*
B: *I do, because I win **more often than not**.*

<u>**Definition**</u>: usually; much of the time; more than or at least half the time.

57. rely on

Situation 1:

A: *Jeremy, you had better get the dark one. It's much warmer in the winter.*
B: *I will. I **rely on** you for good advice.*

Situation 2:

A: *Guys ~ the success of this project **relies on** everyone making an effort.*
B: *You can count on us, sir.*

Definition: to depend on (someone or something); to need support from someone or something.

58. fall behind

Situation 1:

A: *Why didn't you tell me that you're **falling behind on** your schoolwork?*
B: *I didn't want to bother you.*

Situation 2:

A: *I suggest you get this high-end phone. You know, you won't buy a phone every day.*
B: *If I do, I'll definitely **fall behind on** the rent.*

Definition: to fail to meet a commitment to make a regular payment.

59. fall back on (someone or something)

<u>**Situation 1**</u>:

A: *How do you meet your needs with these soaring prices?*
B: *I'm **falling back on** my savings to get us through the hard times.*

<u>**Situation 2**</u>:

A: *I'm not sure I can swing it this time. The manager seems to be stubborn.*
B: *Simon works in this company. Here's his phone number. You can **fall back on** him when you need help.*

<u>**Definition**</u>: to begin to use someone or something held in reserve.

60. devastating

<u>**Situation 1**</u>:

A: *How is your mom doing after her sister's loss. We are deeply saddened by this **devastating** tragedy.*
B: *She's still locking herself in and wallowing in her bitterness.*

<u>**Situation 2**</u>:

A: *Oh boy, the defeat was **devastating**.*
B: *Chill out, man. You'll bounce back in no time.*

<u>**Definition**</u>: causing great damage or harm; causing extreme emotional pain.

Measure your progress

<u>**Fill in the gaps with the missing words;**</u>

1. I have had very little help from doctors and no sympathy …………….

2. There is no logically …………… argument to support their claims.

3. Jane bought ………….. as many apples as bananas. If you had done the same, you could have saved twice as ………… as the money you spent.

4. I was sitting reading my book when all of a ………….. the lights went out.

5. In winter it rains a lot, and more ………….. than not, people carry an umbrella.

6. I'm relying ………… my cousin to fix the car by tomorrow.

7. When some illness persists, doctors sometimes fall ………….. on old cures.

8. The drought has had …………… effects on the crops this year.

9. Never tell them the reason you fell ………… on your payments is because you mismanage your money.

10. Mount Everest is the highest geographical point on this planet, and you can take that to the …………..

Answers;

1. whatsoever   2. compelling   3. twice/much   4. sudden   5. often
6. on   7. back   8. devastating   9. behind   10. bank

Chapter 7

Expressions (61 – 70)

61. swing it

Situation 1:

A: *Are you sure you can afford a new car?*
B: *I think I can swing it.*

Situation 2:

A: *Being responsible for a thousand students is no easy task, isn't it?*
B: Right. *We all hope you can swing it.*

Definition: to do or manage something successfully.

62. take a toll (on someone or something)

Situation 1:

A: *Clare dropped all of a sudden and was taken to the hospital.*
B: *It's apparent that years of smoking and drinking has **taken a toll on** her health.*

Situation 2:

A: *Overusing your phone will seriously **take a toll** on your brain and your eyes.*
B: *I'll try to cut back on it.*

Definition: to have a serious, bad effect on someone or something : to cause harm or damage.

63. home free

Situation 1:

A: *Do you think I can make it to your house without a map?*
B: *I assure you, you won't get lost. Once you leave the main road and cross the bridge, you're* **home free** *- we live just three houses further on.*

Situation 2:

A: *Once the police finish the investigation, we'll be able to make a public appearance, won't we?*
B: *The lawyer told me we're not* **home free** *yet. It's up to the judge to make the final sentence.*

Definition: to be certain to succeed at something because you have done the most difficult part of it.

64. overwhelming

Situation 1:

A: *Are we heading towards the sea?*
B: *Unfortunately not, the* **overwhelming** *majority of students voted for the mountains.*

Situation 2:

A: *What made you major in medicine?*
B: *I've always had an* **overwhelming** *desire to help people and improve their lives.*

Definition: (adjective) difficult to fight against; very great or strong.

65. tread water

Situation 1:

A: *I knew all along that Steve was going to fall behind on his mortgage payments.*
B: *No wonder. He was just **treading water** from paycheck to paycheck.*

Situation 2:

A: *You seem to have totally lost interest in your job!*
B: *Typical. When you're **treading water** with no hope of promotions, you'll end up losing interest.*

Definition: to fail to make progress.

66. at best

Situation 1:

A: *The number of customers in this restaurant is shrinking day by day. Why is this the case?*
B: *People felt they were ripped off. When it comes to the food, it was bland **at best**, and at worst completely inedible.*

Situation 2:

A: *We'll miss the show unless we get to Paris on Thursday.*
B: *We can't arrive before Friday **at best**.*

Definition: taking the most optimistic view.

67. at worst

<u>**Situation 1**</u>:

A: *Jessie was fired without notice.*
B: *Well, she is **at worst** corrupt, and at best has been knowingly breaking the rules.*

<u>**Situation 2**</u>:

A: *The bank will lay its hand on the company if we fall behind on the payments.*
B: *That's unlikely to happen. **At worst** we'll have to sell the house so as to settle our debts.*

<u>**Definition**</u>: taking the worst possibility; under the worst circumstances.

68. marginal

<u>**Situation 1**</u>:

A: *I went for the black car and Simon chose the white.*
B: *Apart from the color, the difference between the two cars is **marginal**, anyway.*

<u>**Situation 2**</u>:

A: *Thank God, the frost had only a **marginal** effect on the plants.*
B: *I covered them all at night, no thanks to you.*

<u>**Definition**</u>: very small in amount or effect.

69. strike while the iron is hot

Situation 1:

A: *The boss wants me to head the department instead of his wife for a month.*
B: *He doesn't often make such offers - I'd **strike while the iron is hot** if I were you.*

Situation 2:

A: *Dad never lent me his car after that smash.*
B: *Ask him to give it to you now, while he's in a good mood.* ***Strike while the iron is hot.***

Definition: to make use of an opportunity immediately.

70. adorable

Situation 1:

A: *You haven't seen my daughter, haven't you?*
B: *Oh, what an **adorable** little baby!*

Situation 2:

A: *Did you have a good time in the village?*
B: *It was great to spend some time with the cattle, and those little calves were really **adorable**.*

Definition: (adjective) very attractive; charming; lovable.

Measure your progress

<u>**Fill in the gaps with the missing words;**</u>

1. Once you get past the essay questions on the test, you're ………. free.

2. House prices edged ahead by 0.3% in February as the property market continued to ………. water.

3. Smoking is at ……. unpleasant and expensive, and at worst lethal.

4. This story is predictable. I think will only be of ………. interest to our readers.

5. Lack of rain is taking a …….. on the crops.

6. Choosing the right software can be time-consuming at best and confusing or frustrating at ……….

7. If you want an interview with Pedro, I could probably ……….. it.

8. Don't wait until tomorrow before you tell him, strike while the ………. is hot!

9. We eventually found the cat in the wardrobe, surrounded by six ………. kittens.

10. Life is hard for nurses on children's wards, where the emotional demands can be ……….

Answers;

1. home   2. tread   3. best   4. marginal   5. toll
6. worst   7. swing   8. iron   9. adorable   10. overwhelming

Chapter 8

Expressions (71 – 80)

71. typical

<u>**Situation 1**</u>:

A: *It's just **typical** of the kids to spend their money on silly toys and then lose interest two or three days later.*
B: *Look, unless you teach them the value of things, they won't grow out of their bad habits.*

<u>**Situation 2**</u>:

A: *Sam called at the last minute to say he wasn't coming.*
B: ***Typical!***

<u>**Definition**</u>: showing all the bad characteristics that you expect from someone or something, often in a way that is annoying.

72. drop a hint

<u>**Situation 1**</u>:

A: *Margaret **dropped a hint** that she'd like to come to the party.*
B: *I won't invite her. She's a real wet blanket.*

<u>**Situation 2**</u>:

A: *Sally was walking back and forth trying to say something.*
B: *Do you think she was trying to **drop me a hint**?*

<u>**Definition**</u>: to suggest something without saying it directly.

73. talk someone into something

Situation 1:

A: *David's room could do with a coat of paint. It looks shabby.*
B: *He's against the idea, but I think I can **talk him into it.***

Situation 2:

A: *Can you **talk Sarah into selling** her car. It's worn-out literally.*
B: *I'll try, but she says she's attached to it.*

Definition: to persuade someone to do something.

74. astounding

Situation 1:

A: *I need to get rid of this car. It consumes **astounding** amounts of fuel, not to mention the repairs.*
B: *Good thinking. It's almost twenty years old.*

Situation 2:

A: *There was an **astounding** 20% increase in sales.*
B: *That is an **astounding** success rate.*

Definition: (adjective) very surprising or shocking.

75. grind to a holt

<u>**Situation 1**</u>:

A: *How is it going at work?*
B: *Once the funding stopped, the refurbishing project **ground to a halt**.*

<u>**Situation 2**</u>:

A: *Why did you allow the thieves to catch you?*
B: *My car **ground to a halt** because the fuel had run out. What can I do?*

<u>**Definition**</u>: to stop or no longer work well.

76. eat away at

<u>**Situation 1**</u>:

A: *Isn't it weird that Jessie is filing a law case against her husband?*
B: *That's typical of Jessie. As usual her jealousy **is eating at her**.*

<u>**Situation 2**</u>:

A: *Don't use this powerful liquid, it'll **eat away at** your car glass.*
B: *Really? I didn't read the instructions. Thanks for warning me.*

<u>**Definition**</u>: to gradually damage or destroy something or someone.

77. eat up

Situation 1:

A: *My electricity bill is so high although I'm not consuming that much!*
B: *You need to replace these non-energy saving light bulbs. They just **eat up** electricity.*

Situation 2:

A: *Man, we're no longer enjoying our leisure time. We're completely overwhelmed.*
B: *No wonder. Rather than loafing around and socializing, we're playing on our phones and computer which can **eat up** our spare time and energy.*

Definition: to use resources or time in very large quantities.

78. uninformed

Situation 1:

A: *Mike got mad at me because I said that his cousins are behind his failure.*
B: *He doesn't want you to make **uninformed** judgments.*

Situation 2:

A: *Oh boy, we paid half of our profits as taxes.*
B: *That's what you get when you're **uninformed** about the tax law.*

Definition: (adjective) not knowing much or having much information about something.

79. knowingly

Situation 1:

A: *What's wrong with you and Steve. You don't seem to be on good terms these days.*
B: *Idiot! He accused them of **knowingly** spreading falsehoods about him.*

Situation 2:

A: *Sorry, Dan. I would never **knowingly** upset anyone.*
B: *No problem. But watch your step and don't make such uninformed judgments again.*

Definition: in a way that shows you know about something; deliberately.

80. fail someone

Situation 1:

A: *How did you know that Albert was lying?*
B: *I couldn't ignore my gut instinct, which had never **failed me** yet.*

Situation 2:

A: *You idiot! You didn't have to say what exactly happened to you and embarrass yourself.*
B: *I tried to come up with some lie, but my imagination **failed me**.*

Definition: to disappoint the expectations or trust of.

Measure your progress

Fill in the gaps with the missing words;

1. It's ……….. of the boss to kick someone when they're down.

2. With rescission looming in the horizon, the country's economy is slowly grinding to a ……..

3. He tried to drop a ………. about it being time to leave, but they didn't seem to take any notice.

4. Unless you get organized, those minor expenses are going to ……….. away at your profits.

5. Christopher was playing happily in hospital last night after making an ………… recovery.

6. For a journalist, he seems surprisingly …………. about what is happening in the news.

7. She doesn't really want to be on the committee, but I think I can …….. her into it.

8. It appears that what I said was untrue, but I did not ……….. lie to you.

9. Words ………. me to thank you for teaching me how to solve my problems without complaining.

10. Multimedia titles, digital photography and other things your kids get into will eat ………. hard disk space.

Answers;

1. typical 2. halt 3. hint 4. eat 5. astounding
6. uniformed 7. talk 8. knowingly 9. fail 10. up

Chapter 9

Expressions (81 – 90)

81. on good terms (with someone)

Situation 1:

A: *Did you and Jessie settle your argument?*
B: *Yep. We're **on good terms** now.*

Situation 2:

A: *Our neighbors are so inconsiderate. They play music at full blast even after midnight.*
B: *Well, I'm blessed to have nice neighbors. I've always been **on good terms with** them.*

Definition: to have a friendly or pleasant relationship (with someone).

82. not to mention

Situation 1:

A: *Steven is always complaining. Is he really hard up?*
B: *Don't buy it. He has two expensive cars, **not to mention** his fatty bank account.*

Situation 2:

A: *Are there other expenses on our list?*
B: *We still have to pay the gas bill, **not to mention** the doctor's bill.*

Definition: in addition to or as well as what's been discussed.

83. literally

Situation 1:

A: *I heard you and Sarah live in the same neighborhood.*
B: *That's right. We live **literally** just round the corner from her.*

Situation 2:

A: *Yesterday's loss was devastating. We've **literally** lost all of our chances this season.*
B: *Oh, man. I **literally** had a heart attack when I heard the news.*

Definition: (adverb) actually; exactly

84. dense

Situation 1:

A: *I dropped Mike a hint to stop talking about his family problems, but he took no notice.*
B: *He is so **dense** - he'll never understand your hints.*

Situation 2:

A: *I'll tell the cops that my employees are stealing money from the company.*
B: *How can you be so **dense**? You'll be taken to jail because you're the manager.*

Definition: (adjective) a stupid person; slow to understand; foolish; unintelligent.

85. wet blanket

<u>Situation 1</u>:

A: *I don't feel like going out. Let's just watch a movie.*
B: *Stop being such a **wet blanket**, will you.*

<u>Situation 2</u>:

A: *David has literally ruined his brother's birthday party. He's a real **wet blanket**.*
B: *If his father had been at home, he would have put a stop to his silly behavior.*

<u>**Definition**</u>: a person who spoils other people's fun by failing to join in with or by disapproving of their activities.

86. grow out of

<u>Situation 1</u>:

A: *Jeremy says he wants to be a clown but I hope he'll **grow out of** the idea.*
B: *Who talked him into this nonsense? I mean it's fun to make people laugh, but not at you.*

<u>Situation 2</u>:

A: *We ran out of cookies. Simon ate them all!*
B: *He'll never **grow out of** this nasty habit.*

<u>**Definition**</u>: to stop having an interest in something or stop doing something as you become older.

87. not to give a damn

<u>Situation 1</u>:

A: *You **don't give a damn** about my feelings, do you.*
B: *Quite frankly, I don't*

<u>Situation 2</u>:

A: *You can't go to the party tonight. You've to get up early tomorrow.*
B: *I **don't give a damn** what you say, I'm going.*

<u>Definition</u>: (slang) to not care about, or have any interest in, someone or something.

88. attribute to

<u>Situation 1</u>:

A: *We **attribute** our success **to** your good advice.*
B: *I'm so glad I've been of some help.*

<u>Situation 2</u>:

A: *What was the result of the investigation?*
B: *The car accident was **attributed to** faulty brakes.*

<u>Definition</u>: to say or think that something is the result of a particular thing.

89. devote to (something – doing something)

Situation 1:

A: *I heard your dad had retired!*
B: *He actually had. He left politics to **devote** more time **to** his family.*

Situation 2:

A: *We need to **devote** all our resources **to finishing** the project before Friday.*
B: *That's only possible if we work on it single-mindedly.*

Definition: to give all or most of one's time or resources to (a person or activity).

90. be accustomed to (something - doing something)

Situation 1:

A: *I never thought I would **become so accustomed to** this dusty old warehouse, but I almost enjoy it here now.*
B: *What did I tell you?*

Situation 2:

A: *Try to do the cooking as early as possible to make time for other important tasks.*
B: *I don't think this will work. The children **are accustomed to eating** late in the evening.*

Definition: to be familiar or comfortable with someone or something.

Measure your progress
Fill in the gaps with the missing words;

1. With these unprecedented pollution levels, we have ………… altered the chemistry of our planet's atmosphere.

2. I began to keep on good ……….. with him since we were in the high school.

3. Come on, Sam. You've become a grown-up. Haven't you grown ……….. of your fear of the dark yet?

4. Those appetizers can be packed with calories, you know, not to ……….. the desserts.

5. The doctors have …………. the cause of the illness to an unknown virus.

6. There are some really …………. people in our class. They want the teacher to stop giving us homework.

7. In the last few years of her careers, she ……….. herself to environmental issues.

8. Now that she is no longer in school, Stella has become …………. to staying up late and sleeping until noon.

9. He doesn't, to put it very bluntly, give a ………. about the woman or the baby.

10. The teenagers don't invite Bob to their parties because he is a wet …………..

Answers;

1. literally   2. terms   3. out   4. mention   5. attributed
6. dense   7. devoted   8. accustomed   9. damn   10. blanket

Chapter 10

Expressions (91 – 100)

91. feel like (something – doing something)

Situation 1:

A: *Sounds like you didn't get along with the new contractor.*
B: *He was so rude, I **felt like** leaving immediately.*

Situation 2:

A: *What would you like to order for dinner.*
B: *I just **feel like** a burger and fries, nothing fancy.*

Definition: to have a desire to do or have something

92. squabble

Situation 1:

A: *Mother is devoted to Dad although they **squabble** all the time.*
B: *There are no exceptions. All families **squabble** about minor stuff more often than not.*

Situation 2:

A: *What's Sam doing during this holiday.*
B: *He's just **squabbling** with others about petty matters.*

Definition: to argue over something that is not important.

93. across the board

Situation 1:

A: *What was the outcome of the meeting?*
B: *They decided on a pay increase of 10% **across the board**.*

Situation 2:

A: *Teachers are arriving late, and the kids are making a lot of noise.*
B: *This school needs radical changes **across the board**.*

Definition: applying to all.

94. pose a threat

Situation 1:

A: *Do you think nuclear bombs should be banned across the board.*
B: *Without any doubt. Nuclear weapons **pose a threat to** everyone.*

Situation 2:

A: *What do you think of the new campaign against drugs.*
B: *I'm up for it. Drugs **pose a threat to** the community through the degrading effect they have on the moral, social, and economic well-being of the country.*

Definition: to create the threat of danger or harm.

95. pose a challenge

Situation 1:

A: *The very high rate of inflation* **poses a serious challenge** *for the working class.*
B: *Well, according to some reliable sources, the government is working on a new regulation to ease off this condition.*

Situation 2:

A: *Lack of tools is* **posing a challenge** *for players during training sessions.*
B: *I was told that the manager will secure them before the weekend.*

Definition: to stand as an obstacle or problem.

96. multiple

Situation 1:

A: *It's a nice offer, but I can only pay in cash.*
B: *That's fine. We offer* **multiple** *payment options.*

Situation 2:

A: *David hasn't been around for a while. What's wrong with him?*
B: *He suffered* **multiple** *fractures in a motorcycle accident.*

Definition: very many of the same type, or of different types.

97. make food

Situation 1:

A: *Dear, I have to stop at the hairdresser's.*
B: *Alright. I'll **make myself some lunch** in the meantime.*

Situation 2:

A: *Hey, Dan. I need to talk to you. Do you have a few minutes?*
B: *Sure. I'll **make myself a coffee** and get back to you.*

Definition: to prepare or to cook.

98. snack on (something)

Situation 1:

A: *I need a good advice to cut down on junk food.*
B: *If you eat three good meals a day, you're less likely to **snack on** biscuits.*

Situation 2:

A: *Are you hungry?*
B: *Actually not. I've been **snacking on** some almonds in my bag all day.*

Definition: to eat small amounts of something as a snack.

99. crappy

Situation 1:

A: *The show was astounding, don't you think?*
B: *Nah ~ I've never seen such **crappy** acting.*

Situation 2:

A: *Why did you take the bus to work today?*
B: *It's better than sitting in that **crappy** car hearing you argue!*

Definition: (adjective - *slang*) of extremely poor quality.

100. definite

Situation 1:

A: *Are you sure I'm invited too?*
B: *Yes, Dan was very **definite** about it on the phone.*

Situation 2:

A: *I'll have to consult my family before I make this decision.*
B: *That's OK. We need a **definite** answer by tomorrow.*

Definition: (adjective) fixed, certain, or clear.

Measure your progress

<u>Fill in the gaps with the missing words;</u>

1. Tom keeps ………….. with his sister about who is going to use the bicycle.

2. The students were deported because they posed a ……….... to national security.

3. In July everything we sell is reduced right ……….…. the board.

4. He died from ……….…... stab wounds to the neck and upper body.

5. Her parents encouraged her to cook and even paid her to ……….…. dinner twice a week.

6. I started working when I was 13, and was used to ……….…. jobs with long hours.

7. October is usually a lovely month in Kansas, but I'll need to check with my children before we set a ……….….. date.

8. One way to lose weight is to ……….…... on carrots instead of junk food.

9. The drought also ……….….. a challenge to the immediate future of thousands of smallholder farmers.

10. Do you feel ………... stopping work to eat something?

Answers;

1. squabbling   2. threat   3. across   4. multiple   5. make
6. crappy   7. definite   8. snack   9. posed   10. like

List of Expressions

Chapter (1)
appalling
appealing
serve a purpose
up-and-coming
down-to-earth
edgy
single out
stock up on (something)
behave oneself
hard up

Chapter (2)
grounded
good thinking
Call someone names
pick on someone
alienate
cut out for (something)
designate as
lay the blame on
hamper
bounce back

Chapter (3)
makeshift
(not) lift a finger
go for (something or someone) – 1 –
go for (something or someone) – 2 –
(get) mad at someone
lost in thought

no thanks to

set off

back off

written all over someone's face

Chapter (4)

engaging

at all costs

touching

set up

rest assured

wear something out

wear someone out

worn-out

give in (to something or someone)

see eye to eye (on something)

Chapter (5)

nag (someone)

not buy (something)

in good hands

resonate with

couch potato

sparingly

in the first place (1)

in the first place (2)

try one's hand (at something)

cross (one's) path

Chapter (6)

whatsoever

twice as much, many, etc.

take something to the bank

compelling

all of a sudden

more often than not

rely on

fall behind

fall back on (someone or something)

devastating

Chapter (7)

swing it

take a toll (on someone or something)

home free

overwhelming

tread water

at best

at worst

marginal

strike while the iron is hot

adorable

Chapter (8)

typical

drop a hint

talk someone into something

astounding

grind to a holt

eat away at

eat up

uninformed

knowingly

fail someone

Chapter (9)

on good terms (with someone)

not to mention

literally

dense

wet blanket

grow out of

not to give a damn

attribute to

devote to (something – doing something)

be accustomed to (something - doing something)

Chapter (10)

feel like (something – doing something)

squabble

across the board

pose a threat

pose a challenge

multiple

make food

snack on (something)

crappy

definite

Other works by the author

Phrasal Verbs (Advanced) The Comprehensive Collection: 1060 Common Phrasal Verbs with Plenty of Examples & Synonyms https://www.amazon.com/dp/B09NGYYCH8

ADVANCED ENGLISH: Idioms, Phrasal Verbs, Vocabulary and Phrases: 700 Expressions of Academic Language https://www.amazon.com/dp/B07RTGWH5X

Advanced English Collocations & Phrases in Dialogues: Master English Collocations with the Aid of Functional Dialogues once and for all https://www.amazon.com/dp/B086JYB24J

Advanced English Collocations & Phrases in Dialogues (2) https://www.amazon.com/dp/B0B752S8S4

Advanced English Conversations (1): Speak English Like a Native https://www.amazon.com/dp/B09PLD4GHN

Advanced English Conversations (2): Speak English Like a Native https://www.amazon.com/dp/B089YTQPTV

Advanced English Conversations (3); Speak English Like a Native
https://www.amazon.com/dp/B0B2SD8TNF

Advanced English Conversation in Dialogues
https://www.amazon.com/dp/B0BBL1HB24

American Idioms and Idiomatic Phrases In Use (1)
https://www.amazon.com/dp/B0BH2W3MB9

TOEFL VOCABULARY (Adjectives)
https://www.amazon.com/dp/B0BD9FR6X2

TOEFL VOCABULARY (NOUNS)
https://www.amazon.com/dp/B0BK9S22RF

Daily English Expressions: Speak English Like a Native
https://www.amazon.com/dp/B0BLHXZJL8

Daily English Expressions (book - 2): Speak English Like a Native
https://www.amazon.com/dp/B0BMYRBJZF

Daily English Expressions (book - 3): Speak English Like a Native
https://www.amazon.com/dp/B0BNGPCVNQ

Daily English Expressions (Book - 4) : Speak English Like a Native
https://www.amazon.com/dp/B0BP5CPPNX

Daily English Expressions (Book - 5) : Speak English Like a Native
https://www.amazon.com/dp/B0BQFMGN6J

Daily English Expressions (Book - 6): Speak English Like a Native
https://www.amazon.com/dp/B0BRWLGYT9

Daily English Expressions (Book - 7): Speak English Like a Native
https://www.amazon.com/dp/B0BSR71WZH

Daily English Expressions (Book - 8): Speak English Like a Native
https://www.amazon.com/dp/B0BTMLFVCN

Daily English Expressions (Book - 9): Speak English Like a Native

https://www.amazon.com/dp/B0BVP8F7N1

Daily English Expressions (Book - 10): Speak English Like a Native
https://www.amazon.com/dp/B0BXBC5L52

Spoken English Phrases (book - 1): Speak English Like a Native

https://www.amazon.com/dp/B0C18Z2X52

Spoken English Phrases (book - 2): Speak English Like a Native

https://www.amazon.com/dp/B0C18X5T1Y

Spoken English Phrases (book - 3): Speak English Like a Native

https://www.amazon.com/dp/B0C3B75NZJ

Spoken English Phrases (book - 4): Speak English Like a Native

https://www.amazon.com/dp/B0C7CM43XC